piano · vocal · guitar

steve green

noel
the *first* noel

ISBN 0-7935-6991-5

CORPORATION

7777 W. BLUEMOUND RD. P.O. BOX 13819 MILWAUKEE, WI 53213

piano · vocal · guitar

steve green

the *first* noel

the first noel

MIDNIGHT CLEAR MEDLEY

It Came Upon a Midnight Clear
Angels We Have Heard on High
O Come, All Ye Faithful

Medley arranged by
J.A.C. REDFORD

"It Came Upon a Midnight Clear"
Flowing, with motion

With pedal

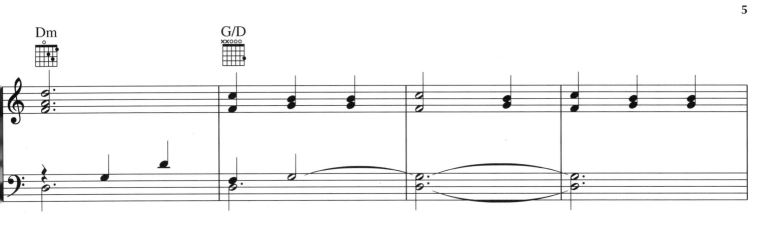

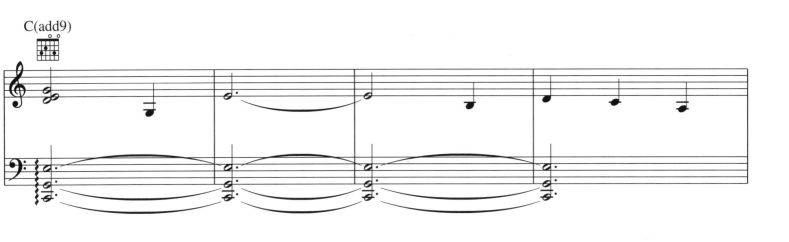

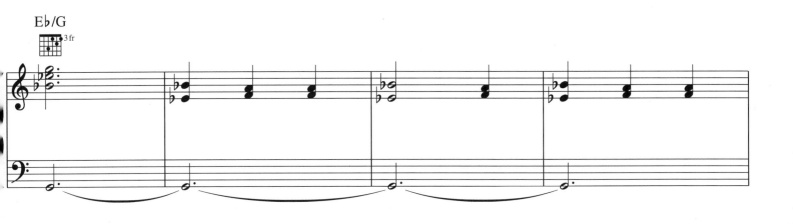

"Angels We Have Heard on High"
Stately

"O Come All Ye Faithful"

THE FIRST NOEL

Arranged by
PHIL NAISH

ALL MY HEART REJOICES

Words and Music by
STEVE GREEN

All my heart this night re-joic-es as I hear, far and near, sweet-est an-gel voic-es. "Christ is born," their choirs are sing-ing till the air, ev-'ry-where, now with joy is ring-ing.

of the Lord. __ All my heart re - joice to - night.

night.

GOOD NEWS

Words and Music by
ROB MATHES

WHAT CHILD IS THIS

Arranged by
PHIL NAISH

COME, THOU LONG EXPECTED JESUS

Arranged by
J.A.C. REDFORD

Come Thou long ___ ex- pect- ed Je - sus, born to set Thy

glo - rious throne.

ROSE OF BETHLEHEM

Words and Music by
LOWELL ALEXANDER

There's a

Rose in Beth - le - hem with a beau - ty __ quite di -

Rose in Beth - le - hem col - ored red like __ mer - cy's

vine, per - fect in this world of __ sin on this si - lent ho - ly __

blood. 'Tis the flow - er of our __ faith; 'tis the blos - som of __ God's __

HOLY CHILD

Words and Music by ROB MATHES
and PHIL NAISH

JESUS, LIGHT OF LIGHTS

Words and Music by ROB MATHES
and PHIL NAISH

AWAY IN A MANGER MEDLEY
(Away in a Manger • O Little Town of Bethlehem)

Medley arranged by
J.A.C. REDFORD